UNITED STATES MILITARY MIGHT

IN THE AIR

V-22 OSPREY

Gareth Stevens PUBLISHING

Thomas Kingsley Troupe

Please visit our website, www.garethstevens.com. For a free color catalog of all our high-quality books, call toll free 1-800-542-2595 or fax 1-877-542-2596

Cataloging-in-Publication Data
Names: Troupe, Thomas Kingsley.
Title: V-22 Osprey / Thomas Kingsley Troupe.
Description: Buffalo, NY : Gareth Stevens Publishing, 2027. | Series: United States military might: in the air | Includes glossary and index.
Identifiers: ISBN 9781482480870 (pbk.) | ISBN 9781482480887 (library bound) | ISBN 9781482480894 (ebook)
Subjects: LCSH: V-22 Osprey (Transport plane)–Juvenile literature. | Transport planes–United States–Juvenile literature.
Classification: LCC UG1242.T7 T768 2027 | DDC 623.7460476–dc23

First Edition

Published in 2027 by
Gareth Stevens Publishing
2544 Clinton Street
Buffalo, NY 14224

Designer: Kathy Walsh/Beeline Media and Design, Inc.
Editor: Tricia Hoffman

Photo credits: Cover, pp. 1 Bob Pool, Flow37 (Swirl Background), Anna Lysohor (Bottom Bars), Kavya/Shutterstock.com; p 4 Petty Officer 1st Class Peter Lewis/Public Domain; p 6 Sgt. Michael Knight/Public Domain; p 8 , 9 Sgt. Tyler Andrews/Public Domain; p 10 Capt. Amanda Mayer/ Public Domain; p 11 Sgt. 1st Class Effie Mahugh/Public Domain; p 11 Iphoto7788/Shutterstock.com; p 13 Jason Johnston/Public Domain; p 14 Nasa @Wiki/Wiki; p 16 Petty Officer 3rd Class Patrick Gearhiser/Public Domain; p 18 Sgt. Meleesa E Gutierrez/Public Domain; p 20 Cpl. Sheila M. Brooks, USMC/Public Domain; p 21 Peter Gronemann/Public Domain; p 22, 23 Senior Master Sgt. Matthew Plew/Public Domain; p 24 Sgt. Niles Lee/Public Domain; p 27 Sgt. Michael Knight/ Public Domain

Printed in China

CPSIA compliance information: Batch #QS27GS: For further information contact Gareth Stevens, New York, New York at 1-800-542-2595.

TABLE OF CONTENTS

CHAPTER 1

DROP-IN MISSION

The aircraft hovers above the trees in enemy territory. The U.S. pilot spots the bright red smoke in the distance. His copilot shakes his head. Red isn't the color they want to see for a landing zone. Red means danger.

The aircraft heads toward the red smoke. On the back ramp, another soldier stands by. She readies the machine gun. The landing zone is going to be dangerous. The co-pilot scans the jungle below for enemy movement. They need to prepare for a quick landing and takeoff.

The pilots check the scanners. Multiple threats are coming. The U.S. soldiers will need to pick up their teammates on the ground fast. They make adjustments and begin their descent. The trees and branches blow violently as the aircraft's rotor blades spin close by. Time for a rescue. What will happen next?

The V-22 Osprey is one of the most unique military aircraft in the world. It's able to fly like a helicopter and a plane. It's the perfect tool to **infiltrate** and **exfiltrate** soldiers. The V-22 is the ultimate transport!

CHAPTER 2
UP, UP, AND AWAY!

The V-22 Osprey is known as a tiltrotor aircraft. It was built to transport soldiers and supplies. It has VTOL capabilities, which stands for Vertical Takeoff and Landing. It can lift off and hover like a helicopter. Once in the air, it can fly like an airplane.

The V-22 has very unique wings. At the ends of each are **nacelles**, which contain the aircraft's engines. The engines power the large **rotors**. The rotor blades spin, creating lift. When the V-22 switches into airplane mode, the nacelles rotate until the rotors face forward.

Helicopter Hurricane

The rotors' incredible power creates **downwash**. These winds can be faster than 100 miles (160 kilometers) per hour. That's as fast as winds during a hurricane!

There are two powerful engines on each of the V-22's wing ends. The cargo area can hold up to 32 soldiers. When it's not delivering troops, it can carry 10,000 pounds (4,536 kilograms) of cargo!

The body of the V-22 can be fitted with armor that increases soldier safety in the cargo bay. The armor can be added or removed based on what is needed for each mission.

Feathered Fisher

The V-22 Osprey got its name from a bird of prey. Ospreys can hover using the wind. They adjust their wings and flap to stay in one place. Ospreys stay in position until they can strike their target, which is usually a fish!

The tail end of the V-22 has several features. The tailfins are attached to the horizontal stabilizer. This helps keep the nose of the V-22 from moving up or down. The V-shaped fins help with side-to-side stability.

The V-22's ramp is where soldiers and cargo enter the aircraft. The back deck is a platform that paratroopers can jump from. They can also quickly **disembark** using a fast rope. Weapons can be mounted on the deck.

CHAPTER 3
A DIFFERENT KIND OF AIRCRAFT

In 1980, the U.S. tried to rescue hostages from Iran. The mission was not successful. Military officials knew they needed a new type of helicopter that could fly far, fast, and takeoff **vertically**. The design work was awarded to Bell Helicopter and Boeing.

The design took a long time. The new aircraft had to be strong enough for a quick takeoff. It also needed the power to carry lots of troops and cargo.

The Bell XV-15 tiltrotor aircraft inspired the design of the V-22 Osprey.

In 1989, the V-22 **prototype** took its first test flight. It was 15 minutes long. The aircraft stayed in helicopter mode the whole time.

Six months later, the V-22's airplane mode was ready. The team worked through challenges and accidents. Between 1991 and 2000, 26 Marines were killed during test flight accidents. The Osprey design work was put on pause for a while. But in 2007, the V-22 was finally ready for service.

CHAPTER 4
TRICKED OUT TRANSPORT

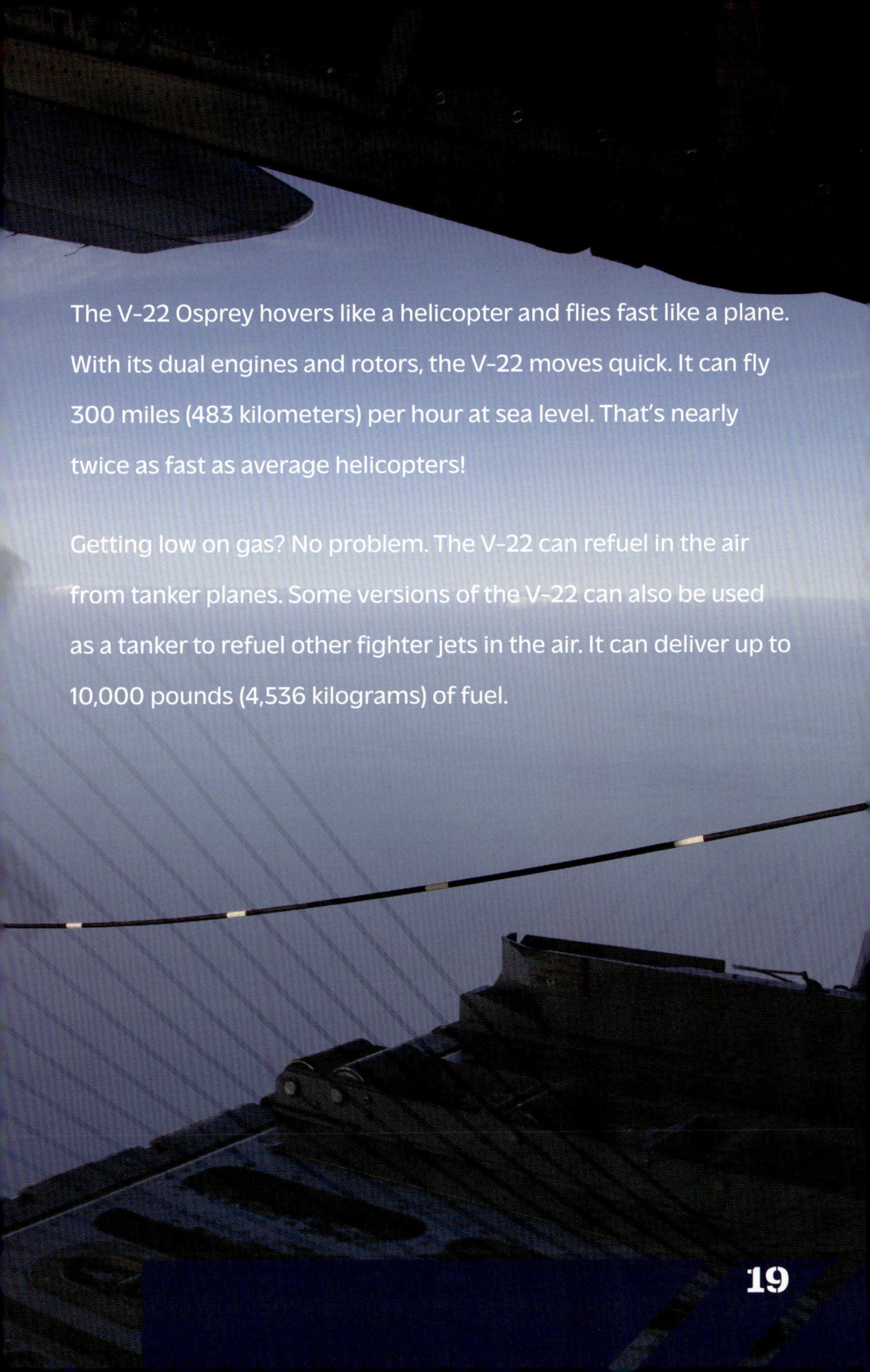

The V-22 Osprey hovers like a helicopter and flies fast like a plane. With its dual engines and rotors, the V-22 moves quick. It can fly 300 miles (483 kilometers) per hour at sea level. That's nearly twice as fast as average helicopters!

Getting low on gas? No problem. The V-22 can refuel in the air from tanker planes. Some versions of the V-22 can also be used as a tanker to refuel other fighter jets in the air. It can deliver up to 10,000 pounds (4,536 kilograms) of fuel.

A good offense needs a strong defense! A machine gun can be attached to the V-22's cargo ramp. Some V-22 Ospreys also have a belly-mounted GAU-17 minigun. It can rotate in all directions. The gun is remote-controlled from a targeting system inside the cockpit. It tucks into the belly of the V-22 when not being used.

Work has been done to give the V-22 more forward-firing weapons. This includes laser-guided rockets. As of now, the V-22 is mainly used to carry soldiers and supplies.

Famous Flier

The V-22 Osprey has made more than 40 movie and video game appearances. It can be seen in the *Transformers* and *Call of Duty* series.

CHAPTER 5

FROM SIMULATOR TO SQUADRON

Learning to fly a tiltrotor aircraft like the V-22 Osprey isn't easy. Imagine learning to fly a plane. Now imagine taking helicopter lessons. With V-22 training, pilots need to learn both! Planes and helicopters fly differently.

In flight school, pilots spend a lot of time practicing in **simulators**. The V-22 simulator is a big machine that feels like a video game. Inside are functions and controls that work almost exactly like a real V-22. Pilots work through different mission **scenarios**. They get a feel for the controls. They spend many hours practicing.

Next, it's time for the real thing. The pilots fly a V-22 with instructors. They'll spend time learning how to takeoff, land, and hover. They will be taught when and how to switch between airplane and helicopter modes.

After about two years, the pilots are ready to fly missions. They will start their careers as co-pilots. Over time, they will be given more responsibilities and different roles.

CHAPTER 6

MISSION ACCOMPLISHED!

When we last saw the V-22 in action, the aircraft was attempting a rescue mission. What will happen next?

The U.S. pilots guide the aircraft down into the clearing. They can hear gunfire. U.S. soldiers are running toward the V-22. The aircraft's wheels touch down on the ground. The cargo ramp is lowered. Rescued troops climb aboard, past the mounted machine gun. When all seven soldiers are aboard, the machine gun fires, keeping the enemy back.

Enemy bullets spray the V-22's armor. It's time to go! The V-22 rises up and away. The mini-gun pops out and fires on enemy forces. The enemy soldiers retreat. Mission accomplished!

The V-22 Osprey is the ultimate troop transport: fast, versatile, and strong. It's a military marvel that gets the job done. Its tiltrotor capabilities, cargo space, and weapons make it an MVP. The V-22 is a true example of U.S. military might!

Time Flies

The V-22 has logged hundreds of thousands of flight hours since the first flight in 1989. The Marine Corps alone estimates that their V-22s have more than 600,000 hours of experience.

A CLOSER LOOK

Aircraft for Allies

There are more than 475 V-22 Ospreys in operation around the world. The United States military and the Japan Ground Self-Defense Force use them.

GLOSSARY

disembark (dis-em-BAHRK): to leave a ship, airplane, or other type of vehicle

downwash (DOUN-wahsh): air pushed down by wings of an airplane or rotors of a helicopter

exfiltrate (eks-FIL-trayt): to secretly escape an area under enemy control

infiltrate (in-FIL-trayt): to secretly enter an area under enemy control

nacelles (nuh-SELZ): streamlined housing for a component like an engine outside of an aircraft or motor vehicle

prototype (PROH-tuh-tipe): the first version of an invention that tests an idea to see if it will work

rotors (ROH-turz): parts of a machine that turn or rotate

scenarios (suh-NAIR-ee-ohz): outlines of series of events that might happen in a particular situation

simulators (SIM-yuh-lay-turz): machines that allow you to experience or perform a complex task by imitating the conditions and controls

vertically (VUR-ti-kuh-lee): going straight up or down

FACT CHECK

1. The V-22 Osprey can change from helicopter to ____ mode.

   a. motorcycle b. airplane c. submarine

2. The V-22 Osprey prototype had its first test flight in _____.

   a. 1980 b. 1989 c. 2022

3. VTOL stands for _______.

   a. Very Tall Or Long b. Victory Takes Other's Losses

   c. Vertical Takeoff and Landing

Answers: 1. b, 2. b, 3. c

FURTHER READING

Henzel, Cynthia Kennedy. *Powerful Military Aircraft.* The Child's World, 2024.

McKinney, Donna. *V-22 Osprey*. Bellwether Media, 2024.

ON THE INTERNET

Britannica Kids: Air Force

https://kids.britannica.com/kids/article/air-force/352717

Check out the basic functions of the U.S. Air Force's functions and aircraft. You'll also get a peek into the military service's history.

Kiddle: Bell Boeing V-22 Osprey Facts for Kids

https://kids.kiddle.co/Bell_Boeing_V-22_Osprey

Get a bunch of facts and background about the unique V-22 Osprey. Learn about the different reasons the aircraft was created. There is also a collection of photos of the aircraft in action!

INDEX

ABOUT THE AUTHOR

Thomas Kingsley Troupe is the author of a big ol' pile of books for kids. He's written about everything from ghosts to Bigfoot to third-grade werewolves. He even wrote a book about dirt. When he's not writing or reading, he gets plenty of exercise. He wishes he had a V-22 Osprey to fly around town. He thinks it might be too expensive and the wind would make the neighbors angry. Thomas lives in Woodbury, Minnesota, with his not-so-little offspring.